BOSTON COMMON PRESS
Brookline, Massachusetts

2000

Other titles in the *Cook's Illustrated*
How to Cook Series

# HOW TO MAKE SAUCES & GRAVIES

An illustrated step-by-step guide
to foolproof classic and contemporary
sauces and gravies.

THE COOK'S ILLUSTRATED LIBRARY

*Illustrations by John Burgoyne*

Boston Common Press
17 Station Street
Brookline, MA 02445

ISBN 0-936184-44-2
Library of Congress Cataloging-in-Publication Data
The Editors of *Cook's Illustrated*
How to make sauces and gravies: An illustrated step-by-step guide to foolproof classic and contemporary sauces and gravies./The Editors of *Cook's Illustrated*
1st ed.

Includes 60 recipes and 8 illustrations
ISBN 0-936184-44-2 (hardback): $14.95
I. Cooking. I. Title
2000

Manufactured in the United States of America

Distributed by Boston Common Press, 17 Station Street, Brookline, MA 02445.

Cover and text design: Amy Klee
Recipe development: Elizabeth Germain
Series editor: Jack Bishop

# CONTENTS

*introduction*

There are many otherwise terrific home cooks who don't know much about making sauces. Whether reluctant to spend the time roasting bones to make a stock or to use the amount of fat required of classic French sauces, or whether simply unsure of what the other options are, many of us avoid the issue altogether, relying on the one sauce we're sure of. But with the mastery of a few techniques—some old, some new—we can add a good deal to our repertoire and make what we already know even better.

Sauces are built using different techniques and are used for different purposes. Skillet sauces, jus, and gravy, which we call pan sauces, rely upon the precious bits of cooked meat or drippings left behind in a sauté or roasting pan after browning, and rescue excellent flavor that would have been lost. Other sauces, like the classic French béchamel and velouté, are base sauces, used to make lasagne, pot pies, casseroles, and gratins. Asian glazes and dipping sauces generally have no broth base, and combine potent condiments with bright and sweet flavors.

I hope you'll use this book in two ways. First, you can explore the wide range of sauces we present, everything from a skillet sauce featuring shallots, herbs, and lemon to black bean sauce for stir fry, to a classic, foolproof hollandaise. But I hope you'll also become confident enough in each basic technique that you'll begin to develop or expand your own interpretations. Once sauce making feels natural, there's no limit to the flavors you can create.

A word on the scope of this book: It covers sauces for meat, poultry, fish, and vegetables. For pasta sauces, see our book *How to Make Pasta Sauces*, and for salad dressings, see our *How to Make Salad*.

*How to Make Sauces & Gravies* is the 22nd book in the How to Cook Series published by *Cook's Illustrated*, a bimonthly publication on American home cooking. Turn to the beginning of the book for a complete list of titles in the series. To order other books, call us at (800) 611-0759 or visit us online at www.cooksillustrated.com. For a free trial copy of *Cook's*, call (800) 526-8442.

Christopher P. Kimball
Publisher and Editor
*Cook's Illustrated*

*chapter one*

≈

# SAUCE BASICS

HE MYSTIQUE THAT SURROUNDS SAUCE making probably scares off many home cooks. However, if you follow some basic principles, good sauces are generally easy to prepare and will vastly improve your cooking. There are three general areas of concern: techniques, equipment, and ingredients.

## TECHNIQUES

A number of techniques and terms are used (and explained) throughout this book. Here's a broad overview.

**ii** DEGLAZING   When you have finished cooking a roast or cutlets, you will notice browned bits clinging to the pan. These bits of caramelized protein are highly flavorful and are the basis for a pan sauce or gravy. To loosen and dissolve these bits, you must add liquid to the empty (and hot) pan. (Keep a skillet over the flame, or put a roasting pan over two burners, as shown in figure 3, page 27.) Because the pan is so hot, the liquid immediately starts to boil. This process is called *deglazing* since the liquid in effect loosens the layer of browned bits and provides a medium into which they can dissolve.

**ii** REDUCING   Many sauces, especially those made with stock, depend on the concentrated flavor and improved texture developed by means of the prolonged simmering of liquids. Most recipes suggest reducing sauces by a specific amount. This is meant to be a general guideline—you should eyeball the sauce rather than pouring it into a measuring cup. Thus, if a recipe calls for adding one cup of liquid and reducing it by two-thirds, you should simmer until there looks to be about one-third cup of liquid left in the pan.

**ii** THICKENING   Thin sauces will run off foods, so sauces must generally be thick enough to cling and coat. Although reducing liquids will improve their texture, many sauces rely on thickeners to give them body.

Butter can be swirled into pan sauces just before serving

to give them body and richness, while egg yolks can be used to turn liquid fat into thick, creamy sauces. For example, oil and egg yolks create mayonnaise; melted butter and egg yolks produce hollandaise.

Flour may be used as a thickener in two ways. It can be combined with melted fat in a hot pan to form a roux, which is then diluted with liquid. As the sauces simmers, the starches in the flour will thicken the liquid. The other option is to blend flour with softened butter and stir this mixture, called a *beurre manié*, into sauces toward the end of the cooking time. We generally prefer the roux because there's more time for the raw, bitter taste of the flour to cook off.

Cornstarch is another popular thickener. It will form lumps if it's added directly to hot liquids. But if the cornstarch is whisked with a little room temperature liquid to form a slurry and is then added to the hot liquid, it will thicken quickly and tastelessly. Cornstarch breaks down if cooked too long, so use it once a sauce is nearly finished.

:: EMULSIFYING An emulsion is a mixture of two things that don't ordinarily mix, such as oil and water or oil and vinegar. The only way to mix them is to stir or whisk so strenuously that the two ingredients break down into tiny droplets. Eventually one of the fluids will break entirely into droplets so tiny that they remain separated by the opposite fluid, at least temporarily. Mayonnaise is an emulsion, as is hollandaise sauce, beurre blanc, and béarnaise sauce.

## EQUIPMENT

You will need the following items to make the recipes in this book.

**SAUCEPAN** A saucepan is a straight-sided pan, generally ranging in size from one quart to four quarts. Since saucepans often spend quite a bit of time on the stovetop, their bottoms must be heavy enough to prevent scorching or burning. In general, we find that shiny pans are easier to work with—it's difficult to judge just how brown something is in a dark pan.

**WHISK** A wire whisk is the best tool for combining ingredients by hand and preventing lumps from forming. A whisk creates a silky, smooth texture that is otherwise impossible. Make sure to buy a whisk with sturdy wires and that the handle is well-constructed and firmly anchored to the wires.

**WOODEN SPOON** A long-handled spoon can be used to loosen browned bits from a skillet that is being deglazed, or to stir roux from the edges of the pan back into a sauce. When the thin wires of a whisk are too delicate, we turn to a wooden spoon.

**▪▪ FINE-MESH SIEVE** A strainer or sieve covered with fine mesh (like that on a screen window) is essential for separating solids from liquids. Bits of vegetable will fall right through a colander or standard strainer, often marring the texture or appearance of a sauce.

**▪▪ BLENDER OR FOOD PROCESSOR** When you want to turn liquids and solids into a smooth, airy sauce, a blender or food processor is called for. In general, a blender handles hot liquids better (a food processor can leak) and also whips more air into sauces, creating a lighter texture.

## INGREDIENTS

The following ingredients are used over and over in this book.

**▪▪ BUTTER** We use unsalted butter in our test kitchen. We like its sweet, delicate flavor and prefer to add our own salt to recipes. We find that the quality of salted butter is often inferior and that each manufacturer adds a different amount of salt, making it difficult to follow a recipe.

**▪▪ CHICKEN BROTH** In restaurants, pan sauces start with veal, chicken, beef, or fish stock. In a nod to convenience, we call for canned chicken broth for the recipes in this book. If you have homemade stock on hand, use it. Stock has more body than canned broth (the former usually contains gelatin from bones) and will improve the texture (as well as the flavor) of pan sauces.

Because canned broth is reduced in so many sauces, we recommend use of low-sodium products to prevent sauces from becoming overly salty. Canned broths from Swanson's and Campbell's (which are owned by the same company) have consistently received top ratings in our taste tests. Canned beef broth is horrid. None of the dozen brands we tried had any beef flavor; use canned chicken broth instead.

∷ WINE Wine is another essential component in many sauces. We have found that it pays to use good wine, but there's no need to spend a fortune. The so-called cooking wine found on grocery store shelves is generally harsh and unpalatable, especially when the wine is reduced and unpleasant flavors are concentrated. In our tests, we have consistently preferred decent drinking wines (priced at about $10 a bottle). Save more expensive wines for the table, where their subtlety can be appreciated.

*chapter two*

≋

# SKILLET
# SAUCES

S KILLET SAUCES ARE WHAT YOU MAKE IN A HOT
pan once thin cuts of meat, poultry, or fish have
been browned and transferred to a platter in a
warm oven. All of these sauces start with the
browned bits and thin film of fat that remains in the pan
once the chicken cutlets, boneless steaks, or fish fillets have
been removed.

In theory, cast iron would seem to be a good choice for
sautéing; in fact, however, we do not recommended cast iron
because it can react with some acidic skillet sauces. Heavy
stainless steel pans with an aluminum or copper core, such as
those manufactured by All-Clad, or heavy anodized alu-

minum pans, such as those made by Calphalon, are our favorite choices in the test kitchen. We like these pans because they are heavy and conduct heat evenly across the entire bottom of the pan. Avoid thin, inexpensive pans because pan drippings are far more likely to burn, especially at the high temperatures needed for sautéing.

To make a skillet sauce, start by sautéing aromatics (garlic, shallots, onions) in the pan drippings. Next, deglaze the pan with some liquid—usually stock or wine, but sometimes vinegar, fruit juice, or bottled clam juice—and scrape with a wooden spoon to loosen the flavorful browned bits. This step is crucial. Once loosened, the browned bits will dissolve into the simmering sauce and enrich it mightily. The liquid should be reduced to a nice, thick consistency—a process that takes about four minutes. To preserve their flavor, we found it best to add seasonings, such as mustard, vinegar, and herbs, once the sauce has been reduced.

We like to finish most sauces by swirling in some softened butter. The butter enriches the sauce and gives it more body. We found it best to swirl in the butter off heat with a wooden spoon so that the butter does not separate.

### ♛

### *Master Recipe*

# Herb Skillet Sauce

makes about ¹/3 cup, enough for 4 servings

➤ **N O T E** : *This simple formula is open to endless interpretation. The basic sauce is best on chicken, pork, veal, or turkey. For sauces to accompany fish or beef, see the variations. Vary the amount of herb based on its intensity, using more parsley, basil, dill, or cilantro and less tarragon, mint, rosemary, sage, thyme, or oregano. If using low-sodium canned chicken broth, no salt is needed to season the sauce. If using homemade stock, season with salt once the sauce has been reduced and thickened with butter.*

½ small onion or 1 large shallot, minced

1 cup canned low-sodium chicken broth

1 teaspoon to 1 tablespoon minced fresh herb

3 tablespoons unsalted butter, broken into several pieces and softened

Ground black pepper

**⁝⁝ I N S T R U C T I O N S :**

**1.** Once sautéed meat, poultry, or fish has been removed from pan, reduce heat to medium, then add onion and sauté in remaining fat until softened, about 30 seconds.

**2.** Increase heat to high, add broth, and scrape skillet bottom to loosen browned bits. Boil until liquid appears darker and slightly thicker (it should reduce to one-third of its original volume), about 4 minutes. Add any accumulated juices from plate with cooked meat, poultry, or fish and reduce sauce again for 1 minute.

**3.** Off heat, stir in herb, and swirl in butter with wooden spoon until it melts and thickens sauce. Season with pepper to taste. Arrange cooked meat, poultry, or fish on plates and spoon sauce over. Serve immediately.

**VARIATIONS:**

## Lemon-Caper Skillet Sauce
Best on poultry, veal, or white-fleshed fish.

Follow master recipe, adding 2 tablespoons lemon juice and 2 tablespoons drained small capers with accumulated meat, poultry, or fish juices. Use parsley as herb.

## Marsala Skillet Sauce
Ideal with poultry or veal.

Follow master recipe, cooking 12 ounces sliced button mushrooms in pan once onion has softened. Once mushrooms have softened (this will take 2 to 3 minutes), add 1 cup Marsala in place of broth. Proceed as directed, using parsley as herb. Season with salt to taste.

**17**

## Balsamic Vinegar and Rosemary Skillet Sauce

Good with poultry, beef, or hearty fish, such as cod.

Follow master recipe, replacing onion with 2 minced garlic cloves and reducing sautéing time to 15 seconds. Replace broth with ½ cup each balsamic vinegar and red wine and add 1 teaspoon sugar with vinegar and wine. Use rosemary as herb. Season with salt to taste.

## White Wine, Mustard, and Tarragon Skillet Sauce

For pork, poultry, or fish.

Follow master recipe, decreasing amount of broth to ½ cup and adding ⅓ cup dry white wine and 2 tablespoons cream with broth. Use 2 teaspoons tarragon as herb. Swirl in 1 tablespoon Dijon or country mustard with butter. Season with salt to taste.

## Port Skillet Sauce with Dried Cherries and Rosemary

Good with pork, beef, or game.

Follow master recipe, decreasing amount of broth to ⅔ cup and adding ⅓ cup port and ½ cup dried cherries with broth. Use 2 teaspoons rosemary as herb.

## Red Wine Skillet Sauce

For red meat or strong-flavored fish such as salmon or cod.

Follow master recipe, adding 2 teaspoons brown sugar with onion or shallot. Decrease amount of broth to ½ cup and add ½ cup red wine and 1 bay leaf at same time. Add 1 tablespoon balsamic vinegar with accumulated meat or fish juices. Use 1 teaspoon thyme as herb. Season with salt to taste.

## Fresh Tomato and Basil Skillet Sauce

For poultry, veal, or fish.

Follow master recipe, deglazing pan with ½ cup dry white wine and either ½ cup chicken broth (if cooking poultry or veal) or ½ cup bottled clam juice (if cooking fish). Add 1 small peeled, cored, seeded, and diced tomato with accumulated poultry or fish juices. Use 1 tablespoon basil as herb.

*chapter three*

3

# CHICKEN JUS

THE FRENCH WORD *JUS* TRANSLATES AS "juice" and refers to a light sauce for meat that is made from pan drippings produced by roasting. Once the roast is removed from the pan, the pan is placed on top of the stove. An aromatic (usually onion) is cooked briefly in the drippings and the pan is then deglazed with a liquid, usually stock. This kind of sauce is generally not thickened with flour or another starch, but it may be enriched with a little butter. The idea is to capture the natural flavor of the meat in a quick, light sauce.

Many cooks may associate the term *jus* with roast beef.

At *Cook's* we prefer a thickened gravy with roast beef (see chapter 5). Since roast beef creates very few pan drippings, beef jus (as prepared in many restaurants) derives most of its flavor from homemade veal stock or demi-glace, which is usually made from highly concentrated veal or beef stock and wine. Substitute canned broth (as most home cooks are likely to do), and the resulting jus is harsh and not terribly beefy.

A chicken jus is another matter. A roast chicken creates enough drippings, especially if you tilt the chicken as you remove it from the roasting pan and let the juices from the body cavity run out. Our goal here was to turn these drippings into a sauce that really tastes like chicken. We had two main questions: Should the pan juices be defatted, and what liquid is best for deglazing?

For our first test, we roasted a chicken and did not defat the pan drippings. The jus was disappointing. Excess fat seemed to dilute the chicken flavor, and the excess fat had caused the drippings to burn in the pan. These burned drippings gave the sauce a harsh quality that was unwelcome. Some or all of the fat had to go.

For our next test, we pulled excess fat from both the body and neck cavities of the bird before roasting. When the bird was done, there was far less fat in the pan drippings. We then ladled off all but the sheerest film of the remaining fat. The finished jus was thin (one taster commented that it "fell off the chicken meat") and not very flavorful.

Clearly, some sort of middle ground was needed. For our next test we still removed excess fat from the cavities before roasting, but this time we left a decent amount of fat in the drippings. (Although measurements here tend to be imprecise, we left three tablespoons of drippings in the pan, and fat accounted for about half of that volume.) We then sautéed an onion in the drippings and deglazed the pan with canned broth. This jus was excellent. There was enough fat to give the sauce body. The balance of fat to pan juices was just right, and the chicken flavor was strong.

We then tested several methods for removing excess fat from the pan drippings. When we tried a gravy separator, we found that many of the browned bits ended up stuck inside of the separator and were lost. The jus made with drippings defatted this way was less flavorful.

In the end, we found it best to tilt the roasting pan so that the drippings flowed into one corner. With a small ladle (the kind you might use to pour pancake batter) or a large dinner spoon, simply skim off the fat that rises to the surface. We found that a small chicken (weighing between 3½ and 4 pounds) produces an average ½ cup pan drippings, provided that excess fat has been pulled out of the cavities before cooking. This means that you should be able to spoon off 4 or 5 tablespoons of fat to yield the 3 tablespoons of partially defatted pan drippings needed for the jus.

Canned chicken broth worked well as the deglazing liquid, but we wondered if other liquids would be appropriate. After numerous tests, we found that chicken broth did the best job of emphasizing the natural chicken flavor in the jus but that lemon juice, white wine, and orange juice can be used to add another flavor dimension. The choice of deglazing liquid is a matter of personal preference and may depend on what else is being served.

Many chef cookbooks suggest straining the finished jus before serving. While this step might make a more refined sauce, we found that the flavor suffers a bit and there's no need to dirty a strainer and bowl.

*Master Recipe*

# Chicken Jus

makes ¹/₂ cup

➤ **NOTE:** *To make sure that the pan drippings are not overly fatty, remove excess fat from around both cavities of the chicken before roasting it. To maximize the amount of pan drippings, choose a roasting pan just large enough to hold the bird. To promote caramelization of pan drippings, roast the chicken in a V-rack. For the best-flavored jus, rub the chicken with a little softened butter before roasting. Vary the amount of herb in the sauce based on its intensity, using more parsley, basil, dill, or cilantro and less tarragon, rosemary, sage, thyme, or oregano.*

|  | |
|---|---|
| | **Pan drippings** |
| ½ | **small onion or 1 large shallot, minced** |
| 1 | **cup canned low-sodium chicken broth** |
| 1 | **teaspoon to 1 tablespoon minced fresh herb** |
| 1 | **tablespoon unsalted butter, softened** |

**INSTRUCTIONS:**

**1.** Remove chicken from pan, tilting bird so that juices in cavity flow into pan (see figure 1, page 26). Place chicken on platter to rest. Tip pan and use small ladle to skim off excess fat, leaving behind about 3 tablespoons partially defatted pan drippings, including all brown bits, dark liquid, and chicken juice (see figure 2, page 27).

**2.** Place pan over two burners at medium heat. Add onion and stir into pan drippings for 30 seconds. Add broth and increase heat to medium-high. Stir and scrape up any browned bits with wooden spoon (see figure 3, page 27), boiling until reduced by half and deep golden brown, 4 to 5 minutes. Add any accumulated juices from platter with chicken and reduce again for 1 minute.

**3.** Turn off heat. Stir in herb and then swirl in butter until it melts and thickens sauce. Serve immediately.

■■ VARIATIONS:

## Lemon Chicken Jus

Follow master recipe, adding 1 tablespoon lemon juice with accumulated chicken juices.

## Chicken Jus with Mustard and Dill

Follow master recipe, using dill as herb and stirring in 1 tablespoon Dijon mustard after butter melts.

## Chicken Jus with White Wine, Garlic, and Parsley

Follow master recipe, replacing onion with 2 minced garlic cloves and reducing sautéing time to 15 seconds. Add ½ cup white wine to garlic and increase heat to medium-high. Boil, scraping up browned bits until wine is almost evaporated, about 2 minutes. Add broth and proceed as directed. Use parsley as herb.

## Chicken Jus with Orange and Cumin

Follow master recipe, adding 2 teaspoons ground cumin with onion. Reduce amount of broth to ½ cup and add ½ cup of orange juice at same time. Proceed as directed, omitting the herb. Season to taste with salt.

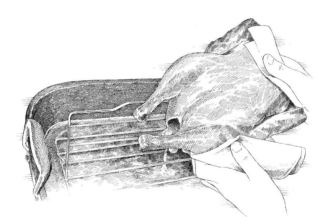

*Figure 1.*
*As you remove the chicken from the roasting pan, tilt the bird so that all the juices flow from the body cavity into the pan.*

**Figure 2.**

*Tip the pan so that juices and fat run into one corner. Use a small ladle or large dinner spoon to skim excess fat from surface of liquid, leaving behind about 3 tablespoons of pan drippings, including all brown bits, dark liquid, and chicken juice.*

**Figure 3.**

*Place roasting pan over two burners to make the jus. Stir the onion into the drippings, cook for 30 seconds, then deglaze the pan with liquid of choice, scraping up the browned bits with a wooden spoon and incorporating them into the sauce.*

*chapter four*

# TURKEY GRAVY

O A TRADITIONALIST, THE THOUGHT OF A gravyless Thanksgiving dinner is culinary heresy. Good gravy is no mere condiment; it's the tie that binds. But too often gravy is a last-minute affair, thrown together without much preparation or thought. Many of us have experienced the result: either dull, greasy gravy or thin, acidic pan juices that are one-dimensional, lacking the body and stature that we expect from a good American gravy.

So we set out to produce a rich, complex sauce that involved as much advance preparation as possible to avoid that last-minute time pressure, when counter space is at a premium and the potatoes need to be mashed, the turkey sliced, the water goblets filled, and the candles lit.

We began our tests by experimenting with thickeners. In a blind taste test we tried four different options, including cornstarch, beurre manié (a paste made from equal parts by weight of flour and butter), and two flour-based roux, one regular (a mixture of melted butter and flour stirred together over heat) and one dark (in which the butter-flour paste is cooked until it is dark brown).

Although most tasters were pretty sure before the tasting began that the cornstarch-thickened gravy would have inferior texture and flavor, it actually turned out to be quite good. Admittedly, it was a bit thinner in body and more acidic in flavor than the roux-based sauces, but it was acceptable.

Overall, though, the dark roux proved to be the best thickener. It added a subtle depth and complexity to the sauce that the other options did not. It can also be made ahead of time, which gives it a slight edge over the other methods, which require last-minute whisking.

To this dark roux, we added turkey stock made from the neck and giblets. Cooking the sauce over low heat for half an hour or more helped develop the flavor, but the resulting gravy was still pale and lacked punch. We then tried using a bulb baster to remove fat from the roasting turkey and using this as the base for the roux instead of the butter. This tasted fine but was not an improvement over the butter version. We soon discovered, however, that the trick was to take this basic brown sauce—prethickened—and enrich it with pan drippings.

Pan drippings are the source of gravy's allure and its challenge. That gorgeous mahogany-colored goo that congeals at the bottom of a roasting pan is one of the best-tasting things on earth, a carnivore's ambrosia. But we found that to get dark brown pan drippings with a complex range of flavors, you need to roast your turkey over aromatic vegetables—chopped onions, carrots, and celery—as well as some fresh thyme sprigs. We also found it necessary to keep an eye on the pan, adding water or stock whenever things started looking too dry.

After deglazing the pan with wine and simmering off the alcohol, we strained the resulting wine sauce into the roux-thickened broth, crushing the remaining herbs and vegetables with a wooden spoon to extract their juices. The result was worth the effort. After a quick simmer and an adjustment of the seasonings, we had an intense and richly flavored sauce that captured the familiarity and comfort of traditional American gravy but that also hinted at the sophistication of a fine French brown sauce.

## Turkey Giblet Gravy
makes about 4 cups

➤ **NOTE:** *For the best flavor, scatter chopped onions, carrots, and celery as well as several sprigs of thyme in roasting pan with turkey. Cook the turkey in a V-rack and moisten the vegetables with water or broth as necessary to keep them from burning. The gravy is best made in stages. Complete step 1 up to a day in advance. Follow step 2 while the bird is in the oven. Finish the gravy (steps 3 and 4) once the bird has been removed from the oven and is resting on a carving board.*

| | |
|---|---|
| 1 | tablespoon vegetable oil |
| | Reserved turkey giblets, neck, and tailpiece |
| 1 | onion, unpeeled and chopped |
| 1½ | quarts turkey or chicken stock or 1 quart canned low-sodium chicken broth plus 2 cups water |
| 2 | sprigs thyme |
| 8 | parsley stems |
| 3 | tablespoons unsalted butter |
| ¼ | cup flour |
| 1 | cup dry white wine |
| | Salt and ground black pepper |

**INSTRUCTIONS:**

**1.** Heat oil in soup kettle; add giblets, neck, and tail, then sauté until golden and fragrant, about 5 minutes. Add onion; continue to sauté until softened, 3 to 4 minutes

**31**

longer. Reduce heat to low; cover and cook until turkey and onion release their juices, about 20 minutes. Add stock and herbs, bring to boil, then adjust heat to low. Simmer, uncovered, skimming any scum that may rise to surface, until broth is rich and flavorful, about 30 minutes longer. Strain broth (you should have about 5 cups) and reserve neck, heart, and gizzard. When cool enough to handle, shred neck meat, remove gristle from gizzard, then dice reserved heart and gizzard. Refrigerate giblets and broth until ready to use. (Can be refrigerated overnight.)

2. While turkey is roasting, return reserved turkey broth to simmer. Heat butter in large heavy-bottomed saucepan over medium-low heat. Vigorously whisk in flour (roux will froth and then thin out again). Cook slowly, stirring constantly, until nutty brown and fragrant, 10 to 15 minutes. Vigorously whisk all but 1 cup of hot broth into roux; scrape any roux around edges of pan back into liquid with wooden spoon. Bring to a boil, then continue to simmer until gravy is lightly thickened and very flavorful, about 30 minutes longer. Set aside until turkey is done.

3. When turkey has been transferred to carving board to rest, spoon out and discard as much fat as possible from roasting pan, leaving caramelized vegetables. Place roasting pan over two burners at medium-high heat (if drippings are not a dark brown, cook, stirring constantly, until they caramelize.) Add

wine, scraping up any browned bits with wooden spoon and boiling until reduced by half, about 5 minutes. Add remaining 1 cup broth and reduce again by half, about 5 minutes.

**4.** Strain pan juices through fine-meshed sieve and into saucepan with hot gravy, pressing as much juice as possible out of vegetables (see figure 4, below). Stir giblets into gravy; return to a boil and simmer briefly to blend flavors. Adjust seasonings, adding salt and pepper to taste if necessary. Serve with carved turkey.

*Figure 4.*
*The pan juices are added to the gravy at the last minute.*
*To extract as much flavor as possible from the vegetables,*
*pour the pan juices through a fine-mesh sieve and into*
*the saucepan with the gravy. Press down on the*
*vegetables to extract all of their juices and flavor.*

*chapter five*

# BEEF GRAVY

OOD BEEF GRAVY IS THICK, SMOOTH, RICHLY colored, and beefy tasting. It should be good enough to pour over the meat itself, not just the mashed potatoes. This kind of sauce was long a standard on many Sunday dinner tables. Unfortunately, many cooks have turned to jarred and packages versions, which are pale imitations of the real thing. Our goal was to develop a recipe that was easy to make and produced delicious results.

Our first thought was to follow the model for turkey gravy—make a dark roux, thin it with stock, and then enrich it with pan drippings. Although this sounded like a

**34**

good idea, it didn't really work. The flavor of the gravy was flat and not terribly beefy.

The problem here was stock. When making turkey gravy, the roux is thinned out with turkey stock made from the neck and giblets. Homemade beef stock is not an option for home cooks when making beef gravy. From previous tastings, we have found that canned beef broth has almost no beef flavor, and we don't recommend it. For instance, when the test kitchen developed a recipe for French onion soup, we found that a combination of canned chicken broth and red wine did a better job than canned beef broth of replicating the meaty flavor of homemade beef stock. Unfortunately, we found that the combination of canned chicken broth and red wine doesn't have enough meaty flavor to work in a quickly simmered gravy.

At this point, we shifted tracks and figured we would start with the drippings and build a gravy in the pan. The process would be similar to making chicken jus (see chapter 3), except that we wanted a thickened gravy. There are three common ways to thicken gravy: (1) make a roux with flour and the pan drippings and then add liquid; add liquid to the drippings to make a sauce and then thicken with either (2) cornstarch or a (3) butter-flour paste at the end.

Turning the pan drippings into a roux was problematic. A beef roast produces minimal pan drippings, rarely more than 2 tablespoons. With so little fat, it's hard to make a decent roux. Supplementing the pan drippings with extra fat solved this problem, but the final gravy was muddy and opaque. Worse still, the flavor was not terribly meaty.

Since we decided not to thicken the pan drippings at the outset, we shifted to the gravy itself and decided to test the two remaining thickening options once our gravy testing was complete. We needed to figure out what liquid or liquids could transform pan drippings into a sauce.

Although quickly simmered red wine and chicken broth created a mediocre gravy when added to a dark roux, we knew that they offered our best shot at creating meaty flavor. We started by throwing some onions into the pan drippings. We found that the onions burned because the drippings were so minimal. Adding some red wine with the onions solved this problem.

We continued cooking until the onions were tender and the red wine had reduced by half. At this point, we added chicken broth. Our first gravy made this way was good but still too bland. It was clear that the broth needed to reduce more. In the end, we found it necessary to reduce the chicken broth by half. Gravy made with this way tasted rich and meaty. We found that the long simmering time breaks down the browned bits in the pan better, so they release their concentrated flavor into the gravy. The individual components have more time to blend, and the result is a more complex gravy.

Despite the long simmering time, our gravy was too thin. Having already ruled out the roux, we tested the two most common methods for thickening a completed sauce: a cornstarch slurry and a beurre manié (or butter-flour paste).

The beurre manié (made by working 2 tablespoons flour into 2 tablespoons softened butter) gave the gravy a slightly thicker texture, but the butter competed with the meat flavor. The cornstarch-thickened sauce was definitely beefier. In addition, the slightly lighter texture of the cornstarch-thickened sauce was a better match for thin slices of beef. Cornstarch also gave the gravy a better sheen.

In the end, the simplest gravy proved to be the best. The key is to make sure to reduce the wine and chicken broth sufficiently to concentrate their flavors and to dissolve fully the browned bits left in the roasting pan.

# Beef Gravy

makes about 1 cup

➤ **N O T E :** *To prevent excess evaporation of pan drippings, roast the beef in a pan just large enough to accommodate it. Also, cook the roast directly in the pan; if the roast is held on a rack, its minimal drippings are likely to burn. Even with these precautions, don't expect more than 2 tablespoons of drippings from most roasts. A particularly fatty roast might produce more drippings; if this happens, spoon off excess fat, leaving 2 tablespoons of drippings, including all brown bits and dark liquid. This gravy takes about 15 minutes to prepare, during which time the roast should rest so that juices can redistribute themselves.*

|   | Pan drippings, partially defatted if necessary (see note above) |
|---|---|
| 1 | small onion or 2 large shallots, minced |
| ⅔ | cup dry red wine |
| 2 | cups canned low-sodium chicken broth |
| 1½ | tablespoons cornstarch |
| 3 | tablespoons cold water |

▪▪ **I N S T R U C T I O N S :**

**1.** Remove roast from pan and place on platter to rest. Place pan over two burners at high heat. Stir in onion and wine. Scrape up any browned bits with a wooden spoon, boiling until wine is reduced by half and onion is soft, about 3 minutes. Add broth and continue to cook, stirring until reduced

**3 8**

by half, about 8 minutes. Add any accumulated beef juices and cook 1 minute.

**2.** Combine cornstarch with water in small bowl until smooth. Turn heat to low and slowly pour cornstarch mixture into roasting pan, stirring constantly (see figure 5, below). It will begin to thicken and darken in color almost immediately. Continue to cook, stirring well to blend, about 2 minutes. Serve immediately.

*Figure 5.*
*Cornstarch will produce a lump free sauce if you take a couple of precautions. First, combine cornstarch and cold water to make a smooth, thin paste, also called a slurry. Then, slowly add the cornstarch slurry to the gravy, stirring constantly so that cornstarch dissolves immediately into sauce.*

*chapter six*

BÉCHAMEL &
VELOUTÉ

BÉCHAMEL AND VELOUTÉ ARE BOTH WHITE sauces made by cooking butter and flour together to create a light roux. The roux is then thinned out with a liquid—milk to make béchamel and stock to make velouté.

These traditional white sauces are not as popular as they once were. Modern white sauces—as made in most American and French restaurant kitchens—rely on reduced cream. Traditional roux-thickened white sauces are not as refined as reduced cream sauces, but they are less rich. We find that these old-fashioned sauces are superior to reduced cream sauces for most home cooking. Béchamel and velouté are essential components in baked dishes, such as lasagne, pot pies, casseroles, and gratins. Cream-based sauces are too oily and heavy in these dishes.

White sauces are bland (they are meant to coat and moisten foods, not add flavor), so texture-not taste-is the real challenge for the home cook. Roux-based sauces are often lumpy. To be successful, white sauces must be silky smooth.

Our first tests concerned the roux. We found that a ratio of 4 tablespoons butter to 3½ tablespoons flour yielded an especially thick sauce—it dropped in blobs from a spoon and was thick enough to spread. Our first thought was to reduce the amounts of butter and flour so the sauce would be thinner. However, we found that in some instances (especially lasagne), you want a very thick béchamel. (The liquid from the tomato sauce will thin out the béchamel, so it must start out very thick.)

More often, though, a thinner sauce is wanted, one that will heavily coat a spoon but still fall in a thick ribbon. Rather than fiddling with the roux, we found it easiest to adjust the consistency of the finished sauce, whisking in a bit more milk or stock once the sauce was done.

In our tests, we found that the flour needs to be cooked in the butter for two minutes to get rid of any floury flavor, but it should never be allowed to color or brown. Cooking the sauce a full 10 minutes once the liquid has been added also ensures that the bitter, raw flour taste has been erased. We also found that using medium heat was key. At higher temperatures, the roux can burn or darken and the starch granules harden and lose their ability to absorb liquid.

Some sources suggest adding cold liquid to prevent lumps from forming in the sauce. The problem with using cold liquid is that it takes a long time for the sauce to thicken. Our tests revealed that boiling liquid will cause the starch to gelatinize and form lumps. However, we found that you could add hot liquid (and thus prepare the sauce more quickly) as long as you add the liquid gradually. As a further precaution, we take the saucepan with the roux off the heat when adding the first batches of liquid.

Whisking the liquid in gradually (rather than stirring it in with a wooden spoon, as many sources suggest) prevents the formation of lumps. Unfortunately, a wire whisk can't reach bits of roux stuck around the edges of the pan. For this reason, you must scrape the edges of pan with a wooden spoon several times as you add the liquid.

Once all the liquid has been incorporated, constant stirring is necessary. Without it, the fully swelled starch can settle on the bottom of the pot and burn. For this reason, it's also necessary to use a heavy-bottomed saucepan. White sauces prepared in thin pans burned in our tests. If you must use a thin pan, reduce the heat a bit.

Béchamel can be used in baked pasta dishes (everything from lasagne to macaroni and cheese), soufflés, and vegetable gratins. We tested various seasonings and preferred salt and white pepper (flecks of black pepper are too noticeable in a white sauce). Nutmeg makes a nice addition for a sauce that will used over vegetables, but it is not appropriate in a tomato-based lasagne. Add this ingredient as desired.

Velouté is a standard ingredient in chicken or turkey pot pies, chicken or turkey à la king, tuna noodle casserole, and turkey Tetrazzini. In general, we felt the flavor of the velouté was improved by the addition of ¼ cup sherry or Marsala. Although we prefer velouté made with fortified wine in most uses, tasters felt the flavor of sherry or Marsala was odd in a few instances (such as tuna noodle casserole), so we decided to make this ingredient optional.

### Master Recipe

# Béchamel Sauce
makes about 2 cups

➤ NOTE: *This recipe produces a thick sauce (the consistency of heavy cream, or slightly thicker), which is ideal for lasagne. For a vegetable gratin, the texture should be thinner, more like light cream.*

| | |
|---|---|
| 2 | cups whole milk, plus more as needed to thin sauce |
| 4 | tablespoons unsalted butter |
| 3½ | tablespoons all-purpose flour |
| ¼ | teaspoon salt |
| | Pinch ground white pepper |

▓ INSTRUCTIONS:

**1.** Heat milk in small saucepan over low heat until hot but not scalded or boiling.

**2.** Meanwhile, melt butter in medium, heavy-bottomed saucepan over medium heat. When butter is foamy, whisk in flour. Whisk constantly for 2 minutes. Do not let flour brown.

**3.** Remove saucepan from heat. Add several tablespoons hot milk and whisk vigorously. Repeat, adding a few table-spoons more milk. Use wooden spoon to scrape roux from edges of pan. Return pan to very low heat and slowly whisk in the remaining milk, stopping once or twice to scrape roux from edges of pan with wooden spoon.

**4.** Raise heat to medium-low. Add salt and cook, whisking often, until sauce thickens to consistency of thick heavy cream, about 10 minutes. Remove pan from heat and whisk in pepper. If necessary, whisk in more milk, a tablespoon at time, until sauce is thinned to desired consistency. Use immediately or place plastic wrap directly on surface of sauce (to prevent skin from forming) and cool to room temperature. (Sauce can be refrigerated for up to 2 days. Reheat over very low heat, whisking constantly until smooth. Thin as necessary with a tablespoon or two of milk.)

**■ VARIATIONS:**

### Sauce Mornay

Classic Mornay contains both Parmesan and Gruyère cheese. Use this sauce as you would béchamel, in any dish where cheese is appropriate.

Follow master recipe, whisking in 2 ounces grated, shredded, or crumbled Parmesan, cheddar, blue, Swiss, and/or Gruyère cheese along with pepper.

### Velouté Sauce

For a richer flavor, add ¼ cup sherry or Marsala with broth.

Follow master recipe, replacing milk with 2 cups canned low-sodium chicken broth.

*chapter seven*

# MAYONNAISE

AYONNAISE IS A THICK, CREAMY emulsion of egg yolk and oil with a little acid and some seasonings. An emulsion is a mixture of two things that don't ordinarily mix, such as oil and water or oil and vinegar. The only way to mix them is to stir or whisk so strenuously that the two ingredients break down into tiny droplets. Many of the like droplets will continue to find each other and recoalesce into pure fluid. Eventually, however, one of the fluids will disintegrate entirely into droplets so tiny that they remain separated by the other fluid, at least temporarily.

**46**

The liquid that goes into this droplet form is referred to as the *dispersed phase* of an emulsion because the droplets are dispersed throughout. The liquid that surrounds the droplets is called the *continuous phase.* Because the continuous phase forms the surface of the emulsion, that's what the mouth and tongue feel and taste first. In mayonnaise, the egg yolk and lemon juice are the continuous phase (that's why something that is 95 percent oil doesn't taste greasy), and the oil is the dispersed phase.

Mayonnaise works because egg yolk is such a good emulsifier and stabilizer. But sometimes mayonnaise can "break," as the ingredients revert back to their original liquid form. To keep mayonnaise from breaking, we found it first necessary to whisk the egg yolk and lemon juice thoroughly (the egg yolk itself contains liquid and fat that must be emulsified). It is equally important to add the oil slowly to the egg yolk. Remember, just a couple of tablespoons of yolk and lemon juice must be "stretched" around ¾ cup of oil.

We like the flavor of corn oil in our basic mayonnaise. It produces a dressing that is rich and eggy with good body. Canola oil makes a slightly lighter, more lemony mayo. Extra-virgin olive oil is too heavy and assertive in mayonnaise, unless garlic is added to make a Mediterranean-style mayonnaise, such as aïoli.

*Master Recipe*

# Mayonnaise

makes about 3/4 cup

➤ **NOTE:** *Each time you add oil, make sure to whisk until it is thoroughly incorporated. It's fine to stop for a rest or to measure the next addition of oil. If the mayonnaise appears grainy or beaded after the last addition of oil, continue to whisk until smooth.*

| | |
|---|---|
| 1 | large egg yolk |
| ¼ | teaspoon salt |
| ¼ | teaspoon Dijon mustard |
| 1½ | teaspoons lemon juice |
| 1 | teaspoon white wine vinegar |
| ¾ | cup corn oil |

**INSTRUCTIONS:**

**1.** Whisk egg yolk vigorously in medium bowl for 15 seconds. Add all remaining ingredients except for oil and whisk until yolk thickens and color brightens, about 30 seconds.

**2.** Add ¼ cup oil in slow, steady stream, continuing to whisk vigorously until oil is incorporated completely and mixture thickens, about 1 minute. Add another ¼ cup oil in the same manner, whisking until incorporated completely, about 30 seconds more. Add last ¼ cup oil all at once and whisk until incorporated completely, about 30 seconds more. Serve. (Can be refrigerated in airtight container for several days.)

**48**

## VARIATIONS:

### Food Processor Mayonnaise
Makes about 1 1/2 cups

Mayonnaise can also be made in a blender if you prefer.

Use 1 whole large egg, and double the quantities of the other ingredients in the master recipe. In workbowl of food processor fitted with metal blade, pulse all ingredients except oil three or four times to combine. With machine running, add oil in thin, steady stream through open feed tube until incorporated completely. (If food pusher has small hole in bottom, pour oil into pusher and allow to drizzle down into machine while motor is running.)

### Lemon Mayonnaise
Follow master recipe, adding 1½ teaspoons grated lemon zest along with lemon juice.

### Dijon Mayonnaise
Follow master recipe, whisking 2 tablespoons Dijon mustard into finished mayonnaise.

### Tarragon Mayonnaise
Follow master recipe, stirring 1 tablespoon minced fresh tarragon leaves into finished mayonnaise.

### Tartar Sauce
Follow master recipe, stirring 1½ tablespoons minced cornichons, 1 teaspoon cornichon juice, 1 tablespoon minced

scallions, 1 tablespoon minced red onion, and 1 tablespoon minced capers into finished mayonnaise.

## Lime-Chipotle Mayonnaise

Follow master recipe, replacing lemon juice and vinegar with 2½ teaspoons lime juice. Stir 1 tablespoon seeded and minced canned chipotle chiles in adobo sauce into finished mayonnaise.

## Garlic Mayonnaise (Aïoli)

Use a chef's knife and ¼ teaspoon salt to mince 2 medium garlic cloves into smooth paste (see figure 6, page 51). Follow master recipe, adding garlic paste in place of salt. Replace corn oil with ¾ cup extra-virgin olive oil.

## Saffron/Roasted Red Pepper Mayonnaise
Makes about 1¹/₂ cups

Dollop this mayonnaise into bowls of fish stew, or use with a seafood salad. This sauce is very similar to rouille, the French roasted red pepper sauce typically served with bouillabaisse.

Mix ⅛ teaspoon saffron threads and 1 tablespoon hot water in small bowl; let stand 10 minutes. Follow recipe for Food Processor Mayonnaise, pulsing saffron mixture; 1 roasted, peeled, and seeded red bell pepper; pinch cayenne pepper; and 1 medium garlic clove, minced to a paste with salt (see figure 6, page 51), with all other ingredients except oil. Replace corn oil with 1½ cups extra-virgin olive oil.

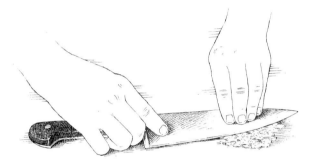

*Figure 6.*

*To turn garlic into a smooth paste, mince it on a cutting board,
then sprinkle the garlic with a little salt and use the side of a
chef's knife to break down the pieces. Keep mincing and pressing
the garlic with the side of the knife until a fine puree forms. If
you own a garlic press, simply put the clove through the press and
then combine the garlic paste with the salt.*

*chapter eight*

# HOLLANDAISE & BÉARNAISE

OLLANDAISE AND BÉARNAISE ARE WARM, emulsified sauces made with egg yolk. Essentially, these sauces are a warm mayonnaise in which egg yolk and a small amount of liquid emulsify a large amount of fat, typically butter. The only difference between hollandaise and béarnaise is the acid used to flavor and help emulsify them. Hollandaise is made with lemon juice, and béarnaise is made with a reduction of vinegar, white wine, and herbs. Béarnaise is considered a more complicated sauce, but in reality the reduction is easy to prepare and can be done ahead of time.

Because they are warm, these sauces are more challenging to make than mayonnaise. Our goal was to create a foolproof master recipe that would produce delicious sauces. Too often these sauces separate, or break, and the cook must start over with fresh egg yolks and more butter. We wanted to make sure that this would not happen.

Classic hollandaise and béarnaise are prepared in the following manner: the egg yolk and liquid flavorings are gently heated, then butter (either melted or clarified) is slowly incorporated. (Clarified butter is melted butter that has had its water gently cooked off and its milk solids skimmed off with a spoon.) Repeated tests with this classic method showed that creating a warm, stable emulsion sauce by hand takes care and patience. Although no single step is complicated, it is a slow process. The yolks can scramble (we found that heating them in a double boiler reduced but did not eliminate this risk), or the sauce can break when butter is added too quickly.

When we got the sauce right, it was divine, with an incredibly light, almost ethereal consistency. Some sources suggest beating melted butter into warmed egg yolks. Other recipes take an extra step and create a sabayon by whisking the egg yolks and some liquid into a light, airy foam. The latter method was key to achieving a superior texture, but occasionally something went wrong.

At this point in our testing, we decided to shift gears and test making these sauces in a blender. Many sources claim that the blender makes foolproof hollandaise and béarnaise that is as good as the best traditional versions. After testing a number of blender recipes, we concluded that blender sauces are consistently very good. While they lack the sublime airy texture of the best handmade sauces, the blender saves time, is easy is to use, and, with its incredible centrifugal power, produces a more stable, firm sauce that home cooks will find easier to manage. A handmade sauce may be slightly better, but the moderate risk that the sauce will break, coupled with the added work that would then be necessary, led us to conclude that the blender is the best place for home cooks to make these sauces.

Blender hollandaise is simple enough to prepare. The egg yolks and lemon juice are briefly blended. Adding a little water helps keep the sauce from becoming overly thick, a common occurrence with many blender recipes that we tested. We found that a little salt and cayenne pepper is needed for flavor. The main area of testing focused on the butter: whether or not to clarify the butter, what the temperature of the butter should be, and how it is best incorporated into the sauce.

When making hollandaise by hand on the stove, we preferred clarified butter. Because butter is whisked into the sabayon, which is already light and airy, the addition of more water from nonclarified butter (whole melted butter contains about 20 percent water) thins the sauce too much; clarified butter, being pure fat, makes for a thicker, smoother sauce. The opposite proved true when making blender hollandaise, where the processed yolks are not as airy. Here the water in the whole melted butter is needed to help to thin out the sauce and make it lighter.

We tested adding hot versus warm melted butter to the egg yolks in the blender. Warm butter worked fine but produced an overly cool sauce. Hot butter is preferred. We found that adding the butter slowly, especially at the beginning, ensures a thick and stable emulsion.

We explored how much butter to incorporate. Many recipes tested incorporated 4 ounces of butter into 3 yolks. We tried six ounces and were surprised at how much lighter and airier the sauce was. We then tested eight ounces of butter, and the sauce was perfect. The additional butter created a lighter-textured sauce.

Finally, we tested the addition of the liquid (lemon juice for hollandaise, the reduction for béarnaise) before and after the butter. When we added the liquid to the yolks in the blender at the beginning of processing, we found that the sauce emulsified more easily. We also concluded that adding the liquid with the yolks early on helps infuse the flavor of the liquid throughout the sauce.

A final note about the reduction used for béarnaise. Some sources rely on vinegar alone; others on a combination of vinegar and white wine. We found that vinegar alone made a harsh-tasting sauce and preferred equal amounts of dry white wine and tarragon vinegar, with white wine vinegar as our second choice.

In the end, we found that the blender produces great results with very little effort. Yes, the sauce is a bit heavier than a handmade sauce that starts with a sabayon, but a sauce made in the blender is also much more stable and can be prepared more quickly. Knowing you can rely on the outcome and count on it to hold up is a bonus.

Blender sauces do tend to thicken and look as if they may be curdling when being held over heat. (We found it most convenient to simply stick the blender into a pan of hot water off heat.) We discovered that whisking occasionally and adding a tablespoon of water easily brings the sauce back to the desired consistency.

▰

*Master Recipe*

## Hollandaise Sauce
makes about 1¹/4 cups

➤ NOTE: *Hollandaise made in a blender is foolproof. This rich, pale yellow sauce heavily coats a spoon—like honey—and should fall from the spoon in a thick ribbon. A classic with eggs benedict, this sauce is also delicious with poached fish or steamed vegetables.*

| | |
|---|---|
| 3 | large egg yolks, chilled |
| 1½ | tablespoons lemon juice |
| 1 | tablespoon water, or more as necessary |
| ¼ | teaspoon salt |
| | Pinch cayenne |
| 16 | tablespoons (2 sticks) unsalted butter |

INSTRUCTIONS:

1. Remove center cap on blender top. Place egg yolks, lemon juice, water, salt, and cayenne in blender and process at high speed for 15 seconds to blend well.

2. Meanwhile, melt butter in small, heavy-bottomed saucepan over low heat until bubbling. Butter must get very hot but should not brown. Immediately pour butter into 2-cup glass measuring cup.

**57**

**3.** With machine running, very slowly add hot melted butter in thin, steady stream through hole in top of blender until incorporated completely, about 1½ minutes. The mixture will be thick and pale yellow in color. If sauce is too thick, add water, a tablespoon at a time, until desired consistency is reached. Serve immediately or keep warm for up to 30 minutes.

**4.** To keep warm, place blender jar in large saucepan filled with hot (but not simmering) water. Keep pan off heat and stir sauce occasionally with large fork to keep from thickening. When ready to serve, remove blender from water and blot dry exterior with kitchen towel. If necessary, whisk in water to thin sauce before serving.

▪▪ **VARIATIONS:**

## Herb Hollandaise Sauce

Follow master recipe, stirring 1 tablespoon minced fresh parsley or dill or 1 teaspoon minced fresh tarragon into finished sauce.

## Mustard Hollandaise Sauce

Follow master recipe, adding 2 tablespoons Dijon mustard to blender with egg yolks and other ingredients.

## Horseradish Hollandaise Sauce

Follow master recipe, stirring 1 tablespoon prepared horseradish into finished sauce.

## Béarnaise Sauce

Great with grilled or sautéed steak, liver, chicken, or fish.

Place ¼ cup dry white wine, ¼ cup tarragon or white wine vinegar, 1 small minced shallot, 1 tablespoon chopped fresh tarragon leaves and 2 to 3 tarragon stems (or 1 teaspoon dried tarragon), 8 lightly crushed black peppercorns, and pinch salt in small, heavy-bottomed saucepan. Simmer over medium-low heat until reduced by two-thirds, 12 to 15 minutes. Strain liquid through fine-meshed sieve into bowl, pressing on aromatics to release liquid. There should be 2 to 3 tablespoons of liquid.

Prepare master recipe, substituting reduction liquid for lemon juice and water and omitting cayenne. Stir 1 tablespoon chopped fresh tarragon leaves (or 1 teaspoon dried tarragon) and pinch ground white pepper into finished sauce.

*chapter nine*

≷

# BUTTER SAUCES

UTTER SAUCES ARE THE SIMPLEST AND SOME-
times the most delicious embellishment to a
piece of steamed fish, some grilled seafood, or
poached chicken. This chapter focuses on
brown butter (melted butter cooked until nutty brown) and
white butter, or *beurre blanc* (cold butter emulsified into a
white wine and vinegar reduction).

To makes these sauces successfully, it helps to understand
some butter science. Simply put, butter is overwhipped or
churned cream. In cream, globules of fat protected by a
phospholipid membrane float about in a suspension of
water. When cream is agitated, or churned, the fat globules

collide with one another, causing the membranes to break. The freed fat globules then begin to clump together, trapping little pockets of water along with the broken membrane pieces and some intact fat crystals. After the cream is churned into a semisolid mass of butter, any remaining liquid is drawn off as buttermilk. So what begins as an oil-in-water emulsion known as cream is reversed to a water-in-oil emulsion known as butter.

All butter must consist of at least 80 percent milk fat, according to U.S. Department of Agriculture standards. Most commercial butters do not exceed this. (Some European butters and Hotel Bar's Plugrá are exceptions, containing from 82 to 88 percent milk fat.) All butters contain 2 percent milk solids, and the remainder is water.

## BROWN BUTTER SAUCE

Brown butter sauce is simply melted butter that has been heated long enough to cause the water to evaporate and the milk solids and fat to develop a nutty brown color and flavor. The key to this sauce is cooking the butter long enough to create that nutty flavor and color without causing the solids to burn. Seconds matter when making brown butter.

We started our tests by making brown butter in a small (8-inch) skillet and a small (1-quart) saucepan. The skillet was more challenging because its wide bottom caused the water to evaporate and the solids to brown more quickly. Everything happens a bit more slowly in a saucepan and is easier to control. It's much easier to watch milk solids change color in a shiny saucepan.

Recipes call for melting and cooking the butter at various temperatures. Although there is a moderate risk of burning the solids when cooking over medium heat, lower flames often failed to color the liquid, and the sauce consequently failed to develop its defining "nutty" characteristics.

We wondered just how far you could take brown butter before it would burn. Tests showed that if you stop the cooking process as soon as the solids turn light brown, the liquid itself is still yellow and lacks a nutty flavor. When you allow the solids to turn a deeper brown, the liquid shifts in color and flavor to the "nutty" stage.

Purists strain the finished sauce through cheesecloth to remove darkened milk solids. The solids do look unappealing, and we prefer to leave them out. A simpler approach is to let them settle and carefully pour off the liquid, leaving most of the solids behind.

Plain brown butter is bland and needs some seasoning. A little acid significantly enhances the flavor of the finished sauce. We prefer white wine vinegar, but lemon juice makes a delicious variation. We found that adding the acid as soon as the butter has browned sufficiently is dangerous since the sauce can splatter onto the cook. By waiting just 90 seconds you can minimize splattering without letting the butter sauce cool too much. Salt and a dash of pepper round out the flavors of this simple butter sauce.

## WHITE BUTTER SAUCE

White butter sauce is a bit more complex but still easy to execute. It is similar to béarnaise sauce, but without the egg yolks. The idea is to create an emulsion with butter and a reduction of flavorful ingredients, usually white wine and white wine vinegar. The goal is to get the butter to soften into a cream so that it forms an emulsion rather than melting to liquid fat and separating. The reduction infuses flavor into the sauce and provides the liquid necessary to emulsify the butter.

Dry white wine, white wine vinegar, salt, and pepper are standard ingredients in the reduction for white butter sauce. A few recipes call only for vinegar, or only for wine, but we quickly dismissed these as tasting unbalanced. In the end, we preferred a reduction made with 3 parts white wine and 2 parts white wine vinegar, with some shallots, salt, and pepper added for flavor.

Some sources suggest reducing these liquids until they have almost evaporated. We found that the sauces prepared with more reduction liquid were more stable and airy. For this reason, we suggest reducing the wine and vinegar by two thirds, but no further. Some sources quickly reduce the liquid, but we found that slow cooking provides for a blending of the flavors and gives the shallots more time to soften.

The biggest challenge when making white butter sauce is incorporating the butter. Some sources argue that the butter should be at room temperature when added to the reduction, while others call for chilled butter. Sources also disagree on how the butter should be added (in small increments or all at once) and on whether the pan should be on or off heat.

Making the sauce off heat failed—neither cold nor room-temperature butter softened. Clearly, the pan would have to be over the flame. We then tested the addition of cold butter in increments over very low heat. These tests worked, but it took 8 to 10 minutes to incorporate all of the butter. Adding room-temperature butter in increments over very low heat reduced the time needed to incorporate the butter to 6 or 7 minutes, but the whisking was still tiresome. On several occasions the sauce broke, probably because we slacked off from the constant whisking.

At this point, we turned to a technique advocated by Jim Peterson in his classic book *Sauces* (Van Nostrand Reinhold, 1998). He keeps the pan over high heat and adds all the butter at once. This method proved easy (it takes less than a minute to whisk in the whole stick of butter) and foolproof, with three caveats.

First, you must use cold butter. Room-temperature butter overheats with this method and the sauce will separate. Second, you must whisk constantly. Third, we found it best to whisk a tiny bit of heavy cream into the reduction before adding the butter. The liquid and acid in the reduction and the water and milk solids in whole butter can successfully emulsify the fat in whole butter. However, some sauces broke when made with only the reduction and whole butter. Our tests showed that heavy cream acts as an additional emulsifying agent. It helps to start emulsification and helps to stabilize the sauce. Our tests showed that without heavy cream the sauce is at greater risk of breaking, especially when the high heat method of adding butter is used.

One final warning about white butter sauce: Make sure that the sauce never reaches a boil, or it will break. If the sauce does break, we have found that the best approach to fixing it is to put 3 tablespoons of heavy cream in a small heavy-bottomed saucepan and reduce it by half over high heat, about 30 seconds. Off heat, vigorously whisk the cream into the broken sauce. Because the sauce loses some of its delicate flavor and texture with this added cream, it's best to whisk constantly at the outset as the butter is added to prevent the sauce from breaking in the first place.

♔

*Master Recipe*

## Brown Butter Sauce

makes about 1/4 cup

➤ **NOTE:** *Caramelizing the milk solids in whole butter gives this sauce its characteristic nutty aroma, color, and flavor. Once the butter foams, the solids brown quickly and can easily burn, so be prepared to act quickly. Adding the vinegar activates rapid bubbling, so swirl immediately to blend. Drizzle over fish, chicken, or vegetables.*

4 tablespoons unsalted butter, cut into 4 equal pieces
Pinch salt
Dash ground black pepper
1 teaspoon white wine vinegar

▩ **INSTRUCTIONS:**

**1.** Place butter in small, heavy-bottomed, shiny saucepan over medium-low heat. Swirl butter as it melts so it cooks evenly. Once melted (this should take about 2 minutes), the butter will begin to bubble rapidly. Keep swirling often until water in butter evaporates (remaining liquid will become clear) and butter begins to foam, about 2 minutes more. Swirl constantly and watch milk solids on bottom of pan carefully. In a matter of seconds they will begin to turn brown. As soon as solids turn to color of dark toast and liquid turns golden brown, remove pan from heat.

**2.** Set pan aside for 1½ minutes. Add salt, pepper, and vinegar and swirl immediately. Let milk solids settle to bottom of pan, about 10 seconds. Drizzle liquid over cooked food, leaving as many solids behind as possible. Serve immediately.

**⸬ VARIATIONS:**

### Brown Butter Sauce with Lemon and Parsley

Follow master recipe, replacing vinegar with 1 tablespoon lemon juice. Swirl in 1 tablespoon minced fresh parsley leaves after milk solids settle.

### Brown Butter Sauce with Capers and Herbs

Follow master recipe, replacing vinegar and salt with 2 teaspoons small capers and 1 teaspoon caper liquid. Swirl in 1 tablespoon minced fresh dill or parsley after milk solids settle.

♛

*Master Recipe*

# White Butter Sauce (Beurre Blanc)
makes about 2/3 cup

➤ **NOTE:** *The trick to preparing this rich, luscious sauce is to whisk vigorously as soon as the butter is added. Fast, continuous whisking ensures that the butter will soften and emulsify without breaking. This sauce is served lukewarm. If it gets too hot it will break. We prefer the texture of this sauce unstrained, with bits of shallot. For a more refined (and thinner) sauce, you can strain the finished sauce. Serve with fish, shellfish, chicken breasts, or steamed vegetables.*

- 3 tablespoons dry white wine
- 2 tablespoons white wine vinegar
- 1 tablespoon minced shallots
  Pinch salt
  Dash finely ground black or white pepper
- 1 tablespoon heavy cream
- 8 tablespoons chilled unsalted butter, cut into 4 equal pieces

**∷ INSTRUCTIONS:**

**1.** Stir together wine, vinegar, shallots, salt, and pepper in small, heavy-bottomed saucepan. Bring to a boil over medium-high heat. Reduce heat to medium-low and simmer until reduced by two-thirds, about 5 minutes.

**68**

**2.** Whisk in cream. Raise heat to high and add butter. Whisk vigorously until butter is incorporated and forms a thick, pale yellow sauce, less than 1 minute. Remove pan from heat and use sauce immediately. (Sauce can be held for 15 minutes by covering saucepan and nesting it in a pot with a few inches of warm water.)

**VARIATIONS:**

## Red Butter Sauce

Follow master recipe, replacing white wine with red wine and white wine vinegar with red wine vinegar.

## Lemon Butter Sauce

Follow master recipe, replacing vinegar with 2 tablespoons lemon juice. Add grated zest from 1 lemon (about 1 teaspoon) with cream.

## Mustard Butter Sauce

Follow master recipe, adding 1 tablespoon Dijon mustard with cream.

*chapter ten*

BARBECUE
SAUCE

KANSAS CITY–STYLE BARBECUE SAUCE IS THICK, sweet, spicy, and slightly tart. This tomato-based sauce is great when brushed on ribs, chicken, and brisket, as well as a number of other meats, in the last few minutes of grilling or just after they come off the grill. We set out to create a quick, thick, smooth sauce from pantry staples. (We ruled out any recipes that call for long simmering times or exotic ingredients.) We also wanted to achieve the right flavor balance of sweet, sour, spicy, and smoky.

After making a dozen barbecue sauces from various cookbooks, we determined that all the ingredients fit into a few basic categories: tomato product, sweetener, vinegar, aromatics, condiments, and spices. We began tackling each of these categories one at a time.

Using our favorite slow-cooking barbecue recipe as a blueprint, we began fooling with the tomato base, trying ketchup, tomato paste, tomato puree, canned tomatoes in juice, canned tomato sauce, chili sauce, and various combinations of tomato products. Ketchup was our favorite, producing a sweet but tart sauce that was thick and had a glossy sheen. Sauces made from canned tomatoes didn't have enough time to cook down (all were too watery and bland) and were strangely reminiscent of marinara sauce

Next, we tested sweeteners. Granulated sugar and corn syrup were quickly dismissed as being too one-dimensional in flavor. Honey was distinctive, but a bit cloying, and brown sugar lost its character in the sauce. In the end, tasters preferred the sauce made with molasses, which added a singular richness as well as a slightly astringent, almost smoky sweetness. We also liked the way molasses colored the sauce.

Vinegar was the next piece of the puzzle, and apple cider vinegar made the best fit—it tasted cleaner and brighter than the sauce made with malt vinegar, which tasted a little muddy, while the sauce with distilled white vinegar was merely tart, with no fruitiness.

Aromatic vegetables give barbecue sauce some backbone. Their flavors anchor the high notes from the acidic ingredients as well as the fruity flavor of tomato. From early tests, we ruled out green bell peppers and celery because tasters found their vegetal flavors to be distracting. Onions and garlic, however, were well liked.

At first we simply sautéed the onions and garlic and then added the other ingredients to the pot. The resulting sauce was good, but we didn't like the chunks of onion floating in the sauce. So we took the next logical step and blended the finished sauce. Unfortunately, the sauce lost its glossy texture and turned into a thick, opaque mixture resembling pureed vegetables.

We were stuck until someone in the test kitchen suggested pureeing the raw onions in a food processor, straining out the juice, and then adding the juice to the sauce. We were skeptical at first, thinking that the process would be too labor intensive. But after trying it, we realized that it actually was quicker than chopping the onion, taking only few seconds to process and strain. This method added a heady onion flavor without the unpleasant chunks.

For condiments, we chose items most cooks are likely to have on hand. Prepared mustard adds a radishlike sharpness; Worcestershire sauce combines tartness with an unusual tamarind flavor; and hot pepper sauce adds a lovely kick of pepper and acidity. We found that too many dried spices give the sauce a chalky texture. In the end, we chose to add black pepper and a touch of chili powder and cayenne for spiciness.

We were almost there, but a little something was missing—smoke. A touch of liquid smoke made the difference between a sauce that tasted good and a sauce that tasted like barbecue.

# Quick Barbecue Sauce

makes about 1¹/2 cups

➤ **NOTE:** *Owing to its high sugar content, this sauce will burn when brushed onto foods over a hot fire. To prevent burning, brush the sauce onto grilled foods during the last few minutes of cooking or right after they come off the grill.*

|       |                                                  |
|-------|--------------------------------------------------|
| 1     | medium onion, quartered                          |
| 1     | cup ketchup                                      |
| 2     | tablespoons cider vinegar                        |
| 2     | tablespoons Worcestershire sauce                 |
| 2     | tablespoons Dijon mustard                        |
| 5     | tablespoons molasses                             |
| 1     | teaspoon hot pepper sauce, such as Tabasco       |
| ¼     | teaspoon ground black pepper                     |
| 1½    | teaspoons liquid smoke                           |
| 2     | tablespoons vegetable oil                        |
| 1     | medium garlic clove, minced                      |
| 1     | teaspoon chili powder                            |
| ¼     | teaspoon cayenne pepper                          |

**INSTRUCTIONS:**

**1.** Process onion and ¼ cup water in workbowl of food processor fitted with steel blade until pureed and mixture resembles slush, about 30 seconds. Strain mixture through

**74**

fine-meshed sieve into liquid measuring cup, pushing on solids with rubber spatula to obtain ½ cup juice. Discard solids in strainer.

**2.** Whisk together ketchup, cider vinegar, Worcestershire sauce, mustard, molasses, hot pepper sauce, black pepper, liquid smoke, and onion juice in medium bowl.

**3.** Heat oil in large nonreactive saucepan over medium heat until shimmering but not smoking. Add garlic, chili powder, and cayenne pepper; cook until fragrant, 30 to 45 seconds. Whisk in ketchup mixture and bring to a boil; reduce heat to medium-low and simmer gently, uncovered, until flavors meld and sauce is thickened, about 25 minutes. Cool sauce to room temperature before using or serving. (Can be covered and refrigerated up to 7 days.)

*chapter eleven*

§

# ASIAN SAUCES

HERE ARE LITERALLY HUNDREDS OF ASIAN sauces. This chapter focuses on sauces American home cooks are most likely to use in their everyday cooking. We have included one glaze (teriyaki sauce), four dipping sauces (soy ginger, peanut, hoisin sesame, and a spicy Southeast Asian version with fish sauce and lime juice), as well as a host of stir-fry sauces.

Unlike Western sauces, which often add richness to a dish, Asian sauces are light and flavor-packed. Most Asian sauces have a strong acidic component, relying on rice wine vinegar or citrus juices. Because these acids are about half as strong as red wine or white wine vinegar, they can be used in substantial quantities.

## STIR-FRY SAUCES

Stir-fry sauces are added to a wok or large skillet (our preference on an American stove, with its flat heat source) full of cooked vegetables, protein (beef, chicken, pork, seafood, or tofu), and aromatics. These sauces must be strongly flavored to give the stir-fry its character.

In our testing, we found that cornstarch makes sauces thick and gloppy. We prefer the cleaner flavor and texture of sauces made without any thickener. Without cornstarch, it is necessary to keep the sauce to a reasonable amount (about one-half cup) that will thicken slightly on its own with a minute or so of cooking. One-half cup of sauce will nicely coat the ingredients in a standard stir-fry for four—containing ¾ pound protein and 1½ pounds vegetables—without being too liquid.

A caution about the use of sugar. Even sweet sauces, such as sweet-and-sour, should contain a minimum of sugar. Too much Chinese food prepared in this country is overly sweet. A little sugar is authentic (and delicious) in many recipes; a lot of sugar is not.

Soy sauce is a common ingredient in stir-fry sauces. We generally prefer regular Chinese soy sauce. However, in sauces calling for a substantial amount of soy sauce, we use a light or reduced-sodium brand. In a pinch, you can dilute 2 parts regular soy sauce with 1 part water to produce your own "light" soy sauce.

♛

*Master Recipe*

# Stir-Fry Sauce
makes enough for 1 stir-fry, serving 4

➤ **NOTE:** *Each sauce will coat ¾ pound protein (beef, chicken, pork, seafood, or tofu), plus 1½ pounds chopped vegetables and aromatics, such as garlic, ginger, and scallions.*

## Hot-and-Sour Sauce

| 3 | tablespoons cider vinegar |
| 1 | tablespoon canned low-sodium chicken broth |
| 1 | tablespoon soy sauce |
| 2 | teaspoons sugar |
| 1½ | tablespoons minced jalapeño or other fresh chile |

## Garlic Sauce

| 3 | tablespoons light soy sauce |
| 4 | teaspoons dry sherry |
| 1 | tablespoon canned low-sodium chicken broth |
| 2 | teaspoons soy sauce |
| ½ | teaspoon toasted sesame oil |
| 1 | tablespoon very finely minced garlic |
| ½ | teaspoon sugar |
| ¼ | teaspoon dried hot red pepper flakes |

## Sweet-and-Sour Sauce

| | |
|---|---|
| 3 | tablespoons red wine vinegar |
| 3 | tablespoons sugar |
| 1½ | tablespoons tomato sauce |
| 1½ | tablespoons orange juice |
| ¼ | teaspoon salt |

## Ginger Sauce

| | |
|---|---|
| 3 | tablespoons light soy sauce |
| 2 | tablespoons canned low-sodium chicken broth |
| 1 | tablespoon soy sauce |
| 1 | tablespoon dry sherry |
| 3 | tablespoons very finely minced fresh gingerroot |
| ½ | teaspoon sugar |

## Black Bean Sauce

| | |
|---|---|
| 3 | tablespoons dry sherry |
| 2 | tablespoons canned low-sodium chicken broth |
| 1 | tablespoon soy sauce |
| 1 | tablespoon toasted sesame oil |
| ½ | teaspoon sugar |
| ¼ | teaspoon ground black pepper |
| 1 | tablespoon Chinese fermented black beans, chopped |

### Oyster Sauce

- 3  tablespoons dry sherry
- 2  tablespoons oyster sauce
- 1  tablespoon toasted sesame oil
- 1  tablespoon soy sauce
- ½  teaspoon sugar
- ¼  teaspoon ground black pepper

### Coconut Curry Sauce

- ¼  cup unsweetened coconut milk
- 1  tablespoon dry sherry
- 1  tablespoon canned low-sodium chicken broth
- 1½  teaspoons soy sauce
- 1½  teaspoons curry powder
- ¼  teaspoon sugar
- ¼  teaspoon salt

### Spicy Orange Sauce

- 3  tablespoons dry sherry
- 1  tablespoon soy sauce
- 1  tablespoon toasted sesame oil
- 2  teaspoons red wine vinegar
- ¼  teaspoon sugar
- ¼  teaspoon salt
- 1  tablespoon minced jalapeño or other fresh chile
- 1  tablespoon grated orange zest

## Lemon Sauce

| | | |
|---|---|---|
| 3 | tablespoons lemon juice |
| ½ | teaspoon minced lemon zest |
| 2 | tablespoons canned low-sodium chicken broth |
| 1 | tablespoon soy sauce |
| 2 | teaspoons sugar |

■■ INSTRUCTIONS:

1. For each stir-fry sauce, combine all ingredients in small bowl and set aside until needed. (Sauces can be prepared a few hours in advance.)

2. Once all ingredients have been stir-fried, add sauce to pan along with any ingredients that have been stir-fried and then removed from pan. Stir-fry until ingredients are well coated with sauce and sizzling hot, about 1 minute.

GLAZING SAUCE

Teriyaki sauce is a Japanese sauce made from mirin (sweet Japanese rice wine), soy sauce, sugar, and (often) sake. Teriyaki is typically used in two ways. Usually it is brushed on foods as they grill or broil. The sauce coats foods and forms a syrupy, crusty glaze. Teriyaki sauce can also be used as a finishing sauce in a hot skillet. In Japanese cooking, it is sometimes poured over a piece of beef or salmon that has been pan-fried. The sauce reduces briefly to coat the meat or fish with a shiny glaze.

Some sources suggest using just soy and mirin to make teriyaki. In our testing, we preferred sauces made with sake, which balances the salty soy and sweet mirin. We found it necessary to simmer the sauce—some sources suggest just mixing the ingredients together—to dissolve the sugar and thicken the texture. If not reduced substantially, the sauce will run off foods and create flare-ups when grilling.

# Teriyaki Sauce
makes about ¼ cup

➤ NOTE: *This sweet and salty Japanese sauce can be used with fish, meat, or poultry. Because the soy sauce provides salt, do not salt the protein beforehand. This recipe yields enough sauce for 4 to 6 portions of protein.*

| | |
|---|---|
| ¼ | cup soy sauce |
| ¼ | cup mirin |
| ¼ | cup sake |
| 1 | tablespoon sugar |

⸬ INSTRUCTIONS:

**1.** Combine ingredients in small, heavy-bottomed saucepan and cook over medium heat until sugar dissolves, about 1 minute. Raise heat to high and simmer until mixture is thick and syrupy and has reduced by two-thirds, 5 to 6 minutes. Remove pan from heat and cool. (Sauce can be refrigerated in airtight container for 1 month.)

**2.** To use, brush directly on grilled or broiled food during last minute of cooking. Brush again prior to serving.

**VARIATION:**
### Teriyaki Pan Sauce
The pan sauce is prepared while the fish, meat, or poultry is still in the pan.

Combine all ingredients for Teriyaki Sauce in small bowl. When protein is browned on both sides but underdone by about 3 minutes, pour off any excess oil and add teriyaki liquid and undissolved sugar. Cook over medium-high heat for 1½ minutes. Turn protein and cook until liquid is thick and syrupy and just a few tablespoons remain, about 1 minute. Transfer cooked protein to platter and drizzle with pan sauce. Serve immediately.

### DIPPING SAUCES

Dipping sauces are fairly easy to construct. Since they are used on the table and most of the sauce will fall back into the bowl, they must be potent. A little sauce has to go a long way. The other main consideration is consistency. Thicker sauces adhere best to skewers of beef or chicken. Since more sauce ends up in our mouth, these sauces tend toward the sweet. A thinner sauce is fine for dumplings or spring rolls, which will absorb some of the sauce. Highly acidic or salty sauces are generally thin so that they don't overwhelm foods.

## Soy Ginger Dipping Sauce
### makes about 1 cup

➤ **NOTE:** *Serve this thin, salty sauce with dumplings or potstickers.*

| | |
|---|---|
| ¼ | cup soy sauce |
| ¼ | cup rice wine vinegar |
| 2½ | teaspoons sugar |
| ½ | medium scallion, minced |
| 2 | teaspoons minced fresh gingerroot |
| ½ | teaspoon toasted sesame oil |
| ½ | teaspoon hot red pepper flakes |

**INSTRUCTIONS:**

**1.** Bring soy sauce, vinegar, sugar, and ¼ cup water to boil in small saucepan over medium heat, stirring until sugar dissolves.

**84**

**2.** Pour mixture into bowl and stir in scallion, ginger, oil, and hot red pepper flakes. (Sauce can be refrigerated in airtight container for several days.)

## Spicy Southeast Asian Dipping Sauce
makes about ¹/2 cup

➤ NOTE: *This tart, thin sauce is a common component of meals in Vietnam and Thailand. It can be used as a dipping sauce with rice paper spring rolls, grilled or poached seafood (especially shrimp), or grilled chicken. This refreshing sauce makes a wonderful dressing for salads or slaws containing napa cabbage, cucumbers, carrots, and the Southeast Asian trilogy of herbs—mint, basil, and cilantro. If using as a dressing, mince the garlic and use just half a clove; also, eliminate the grated carrot in salads with carrot.*

- ¼ cup lime juice
- 2 tablespoons fish sauce
- 1 tablespoon sugar
- 1 large garlic clove, thinly sliced
- ½ small carrot, peeled and coarsely grated
- ¼ teaspoon hot red pepper flakes

**INSTRUCTIONS:**

Mix all ingredients for sauce together in small bowl. Set aside, stirring occasionally to dissolve sugar, until flavors develop, at least 1 hour or up to 1 day.

**85**

# Spicy Peanut Dipping Sauce
makes about $3/4$ cup

➤ **NOTE:** *Serve this thick sauce with grilled chicken, grilled shrimp, or Thai spring rolls. You can also thin this sauce with stock or cooking water and then toss with Chinese egg noodles. Soy sauce is traditional in Chinese versions of this sauce; fish sauce is characteristic of Thai cooking.*

| | |
|---|---|
| 5 | tablespoons creamy peanut butter |
| ¼ | cup unsweetened coconut milk |
| 2 | tablespoons lime juice |
| 1 | tablespoon honey |
| 2 | teaspoons soy sauce or fish sauce |
| 1 | tablespoon minced fresh gingerroot |
| 2 | medium garlic cloves, minced |
| ½ | teaspoon red pepper flakes |

**INSTRUCTIONS:**

Place all ingredients in blender or food processor and process until smooth. (Sauce can be refrigerated in airtight container for several days.)

# Hoisin Sesame Dipping Sauce

makes about ¹/₂ cup

➤ **NOTE:** *This sweet, thick sauce works well with dumplings and grilled chicken wings as well as with skewered grilled chicken, beef, shrimp, or scallops.*

| | |
|---|---|
| 2 | tablespoons hoisin sauce |
| 1 | tablespoon rice wine vinegar |
| 1 | tablespoon soy sauce |
| 1 | teaspoon toasted sesame oil |
| 1 | tablespoon vegetable oil |
| 2 | tablespoons minced fresh gingerroot |
| 2 | medium garlic cloves, minced |
| 2 | tablespoons chopped fresh cilantro leaves |

**INSTRUCTIONS:**

1. Mix hoisin sauce, vinegar, soy sauce, sesame oil, and 2 tablespoons water in small bowl; set aside.

2. Heat vegetable oil in small saucepan over medium heat. Add ginger and garlic and sauté until fragrant but not browned, about 30 seconds. Stir in hoisin mixture; cook until flavors meld, 2 to 3 minutes. Off heat, stir in cilantro. Serve warm or at room temperature. (Sauce can be refrigerated in airtight container for several days.)

*chapter twelve*

# VEGETABLE
# PUREES & SAUCES

THESE MODERN SAUCES DERIVE THEIR TEXture and flavor from vegetables or from fruits used in savory cooking, such as tomatoes. Classic sauces rely on fat (in the form of butter, eggs, cream) or flour for body. In recent years, chefs have turned to "meaty" vegetables such as carrots and red bell peppers to create texture. The resulting sauces are packed with flavor and generally low in fat.

When pureeing ingredients to make a sauce, we find that the blender creates a smoother texture, although a food processor can also be used. Some sauces in this chapter are not pureed; rather, they are "chunky," with most of the liquid cooked off so the sauce is not too runny. Recipes in this chapter yield enough sauce for four to six generous servings.

**88**

# Red Pepper Sauce with Basil
makes about 1 cup

➤ NOTE: *Most pureed bell pepper sauces call for roasted, peeled peppers. In this recipe, diced raw peppers are sweated in a covered pan until very tender and then pureed to create a rich, thick sauce. Serve with pork, chicken, or white-fleshed fish.*

| | |
|---|---|
| 1½ | tablespoons extra-virgin olive oil |
| 1 | small onion, chopped |
| 1 | large red bell pepper, cored, seeded, and chopped |
| ½ | cup canned low-sodium chicken broth |
| 1 | medium garlic clove, minced |
| 2 | tablespoons minced fresh basil leaves |
| 1–2 | teaspoons balsamic vinegar |
| | Salt and ground black pepper |

▓ INSTRUCTIONS:

1. Heat oil in small saucepan over medium heat. Add onion and sauté until softened, about 3 minutes. Reduce heat to low. Add red pepper, cover, and cook, stirring frequently, until very tender, 15 to 20 minutes.

2. Transfer mixture to blender or food processor. Add stock and process until smooth. Return mixture to saucepan. Add garlic and simmer to blend flavors, about 5 minutes. (Sauce can be refrigerated in airtight container for several days.) When ready to serve, heat sauce and stir in basil and season to taste with vinegar, salt, and pepper.

# Carrot-Ginger Sauce

## Makes about 1 1/2 cups

➤ NOTE: *Pungent ginger juice and pureed sweet carrots combine to create this brightly colored and flavorful sauce. Serve with fish, chicken, or pork.*

| | |
|---|---|
| 1 | tablespoon unsalted butter |
| ½ | small onion, minced |
| 2 | medium carrots, peeled and cut in 1-inch chunks |
| ½ | cup canned low-sodium chicken broth |
| ¼ | cup dry white wine |
| 1 | tablespoon juice from 2-inch piece fresh gingerroot (see figures 7 and 8, page 91) |
| 1 | teaspoon white wine vinegar |
| | Salt and ground white pepper |

**INSTRUCTIONS:**

**1.** Heat butter in saucepan over low heat. Add onion and sauté until softened, 3 to 4 minutes. Add carrots, broth, and wine; increase heat to high and bring to boil. Reduce heat to low, cover, and cook until carrots are very tender, 15 to 20 minutes.

**2.** Transfer carrot mixture to blender or food processor and process until smooth. Pulse in ginger juice, vinegar, and salt and pepper to taste. If sauce is too thick, add hot water, 1 tablespoon at a time. (Sauce can be refrigerated in airtight container for up to 1 week.)

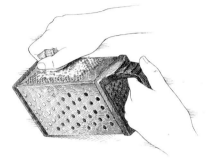

*Figure 7.*
*Grate unpeeled knob of gingerroot against fine holes on a box grater.*

*Figure 8.*
*Wrap grated ginger in a double layer of cheesecloth. Squeeze*
*tightly over a small bowl to extract juice.*

# Porcini Mushroom/Red Wine Sauce

makes about 2 cups

➤ **NOTE:** *Use dried porcini that are large, thick, and tan or brown in color. Rehydrating the mushrooms takes some time and effort, but the reward is an intensely flavored liquid that is used to make this earthy, robust sauce. Serve with red meat and mashed potatoes or rice.*

| | |
|---|---|
| 2 | ounces dried porcini mushrooms |
| 2 | cups hot water |
| 2 | tablespoons unsalted butter |
| 1 | small onion, minced |
| | Salt and ground black pepper |
| 1 | tablespoon cornstarch |
| 1 | cup dry red wine |
| 2 | tablespoons minced fresh parsley leaves |

**INSTRUCTIONS:**

**1.** Place porcini in small bowl, cover with hot water, and soak until softened, about 20 minutes. Lift porcini from water with fork. If they feel gritty, rinse under cold water. Trim any tough stems and chop porcini. Strain soaking liquid through sieve lined with paper towel and reserve separately.

**2.** Heat butter over medium-low heat in medium saucepan. Add onion and sauté until translucent, about 5 minutes.

Add chopped porcini; sauté to release flavors, 1 to 2 minutes. Season with salt and pepper to taste.

**3.** Meanwhile, mix cornstarch with 2 tablespoons reserved soaking liquid in small bowl until smooth. Add remaining soaking liquid and wine to saucepan; increase heat to medium and simmer briskly until liquid has reduced by two-thirds, about 15 minutes.

**4.** Reblend cornstarch mixture and stir into saucepan. Cook until liquid has thickened and darkened, 1 to 2 minutes. Stir in parsley, adjust seasonings, and serve. (Sauce can be refrigerated in airtight container for several days.)

# Tomatillo-Chile Sauce

makes about 1 cup

➤ **NOTE:** *Serve this tart, fragrant sauce with seafood, grilled beef, pork, or even chicken.*

|       |                                                                        |
|-------|------------------------------------------------------------------------|
| ½     | pound fresh tomatillos, husked and washed                              |
| 1–2   | fresh jalapeño or serrano chiles, stemmed (and seeded for a milder sauce) |
| 2     | tablespoons chopped fresh cilantro leaves                              |
| ½     | small onion, chopped                                                    |
| 1     | small garlic clove, chopped                                            |
| 1½    | teaspoons vegetable oil                                                 |
| ½     | cup canned low-sodium chicken broth                                     |
|       | Salt                                                                    |

**INSTRUCTIONS:**

**1.** Place tomatillos and chiles in saucepan; add water to cover. Bring to a boil, cover, and simmer until barely tender, about 8 minutes. Drain and transfer to food processor or blender. Add cilantro, onion, and garlic and pulse to coarse puree.

**2.** Heat oil in medium skillet until shimmering. Add puree all at once and cook, stirring often, over medium-high heat, until mixture darkens and thickens, about 5 minutes. Add broth and simmer, stirring occasionally, until mixture thickens, 10 to 15 minutes. Season with salt to taste. (Sauce can be refrigerated in airtight container for 2 days).

# *index*

*Index continued on next page*